THE DEVIL SOLD US A DUMMY

(AND WE'RE STILL TRYING TO FLIP IT)

STEWART BROCKENBROUGH

Copyright © 2016 Stewart Brockenbrough

All rights reserved.

ISBN: 1542544874
ISBN-13: 978-1542544870

Website: thedevilsoldusadummy.com
Cover: Robins Dotter
Typesetting: Vic King

DEDICATION

To Daiarei -
When I lost my faith, you restored it!
Thanks Lil' Brah

CONTENTS

Dedication

1. Alpha   3
2. The Entrepreneur   13
3. Whose Child Are You?   19
4. John 10:10 Pt 1   27
5. Right or Wrong   47
6. What Am I Promised?   65
7. "Both Black And White"   71
8. John 10:10 Pt 2   79
9. Omega   87

About the Author

dummy *duh-me*\ n. fake substance being made to look or feel like the real thing

2. Fake drugs sold as the real thing

3. Anything other than, or in opposition to what God thinks and/or says concerning your life or your purpose

> "Or is it the one I beat for 5,000 dollars / Thought he had 'caine but it was Gold Medal flour"

flip *flip*\ v. turn something into [a] profit
> ex: He earned one thousand dollars in one weekend flipping cars.

"But if the gospel be hid, it is hid to them that are lost: In whom the god of this world hath blinded the minds of them which believe not, lest the glorious gospel of Christ, who is the image of God, should shine unto them."

2 Corinthians 4:3-4

ALPHA

I've always considered myself to be fair and just. That's not to say that I haven't done my share of wrong like most humans, maybe more, but I feel that they have always been two character traits of mine. That's the way God made me when (or before) He formed me in my mother's womb (Jeremiah 1:5). I wonder, had I used those traits to do the right thing, where they would've taken me. Where were they supposed to take me, or what impact was I supposed to have on the world given the fact that those were my two gifts? Was I supposed to be a judge?

Maybe I was supposed to be some sort of mediator, who knows? The real question is: did the enemy (the devil) trick me, through careful plotting and manipulation, and make me believe that I was a drug dealer, or a thug, or any of the other things that I thought I was? Maybe I was supposed to be a congressman or a part of the senate. Then I would be able to help the judicial system rather than sitting back complaining about what I feel is unfair or unjust.

Those are just two of my character traits, or better yet gifts, what about you? What are yours? Who are you really? There are some things I didn't know about myself until I came out of the haze of marijuana, and liquor, and pills, or anything else that had warped my way of thinking, and really sat back and got a clear look at myself. Do you think it's a coincidence people's thoughts start to get clearer when they are sober, whether by choice, like quitting on their own, or by force, like being locked up?

At nineteen years old I went to the state penitentiary in Virginia, for the first time, for a 3 year sentence. While there I got a tattoo on my left shoulder—a picture of hands praying. One of the hands is normal, the other the bones of the fingers can be seen with the skin hanging off, and the title "Unanswered Prayers" written above it. What made me come up with that was the thought of all of the people who had chosen the streets, who had died or gone to prison for a large amount of time without ever experiencing the things the streets were promising us. It was more symbolic of those things than the actual thought that the prayers were really unanswered. Now I can see where prayers are definitely answered and that things happen for a reason. As you can see, the streets, and the effect it has had on us, has always been something that I have been passionate about, even while I was a part of it. I can say that at that time, and at that age, I was struggling with my belief and how it all coincided with my life. When I say my life, I'm referring to me at the time being a black teen, all that I had seen in my younger years, the street theory that I had adapted and believed in, even the superstitions that I believed in (such as don't split the pole because it's bad luck and all those types of things). Those being some of the main things, but also every other thing that made me who I was at the time; who I was becoming.

Even though my "Unanswered Prayers" tattoo really had nothing to do with my faith, at that time my faith was not where it should've been, which left an opening. Not being as solid as I needed to be in that area, I took in a lot. Some of what I took in was the thoughts and ideas of other people who were relatable, because of my perceptions, like I see many people do. This steered my beliefs. Not that I was just open to anything, but I was open to anything; unprotected. Most of the reason that I was unprotected (spiritually) is because I was searching for something to validate or come close to what I was feeling, or give an answer to what I was feeling. For example: being passionate about, while also going through, the plight of black men, led to the fact that if a person was speaking on the topic in a way that seemed right, I would give an ear to it. If it seemed to have merit, if it seemed to be edifying or helpful to my young mind, then why not give an ear to it. The devil operates that way. Like I told you, I was already passionate about these things, and not being fully grounded (or being unprotected like I said earlier), the enemy was able to use my passions against me. Whenever we're not on point (not focused) we allow an entry point or we give the enemy an access point into our lives. One of the things I started studying was a thing called "knowledge of self", or being known as a "five percenter". On a small scale some of their beliefs are that there is no spiritual or mystical God in the sky, and that the black man is "god", and much, much more.

They made it sound right, believe me. Especially to a black teen feeling the pressure of just being a black teen, and not having anything to dispute what was being told to me. It seemed right. It seemed like I was really believing in a false made up god in the sky that the slave owners had given to us to trick us, and that atoms had mysteriously come together and formed everything, even man. That the black man was god because of the melanin in our skin, and whatever other convincing theory they were giving me to support their thesis. So I started leaning towards their beliefs. I started to believe in what "seemed" right, and what agreed with my soul. I see it daily, especially with the rise in police attacks and the racism that continues to plague the nation. Our soul (thoughts, feelings, and emotions) feels the immediate need to lash back. Romans 12:19 says "Dear beloved, avenge not yourselves, but rather give place unto wrath: for it is written, Vengeance is mine; I will repay, saith the Lord." God will defend the cause. God will "defend the poor and the fatherless, and do justice to the afflicted and the needy, defend the poor and needy: rid them out of the hand of the wicked" (Psalm 82:3-4). In the scripture before that, in Psalm 82:2, the psalmist asks "How long will ye judge unjustly, and accept the persons of the wicked?" He's asking how long will you allow this to be Lord, how long will you tolerate the wicked. That shows that even during those times the people of God had to wait on God, but the person didn't give up and take matters into his own hand. He was waiting on the Lord to come through. That's faith!!! That's what faith is all about! It's knowing that God can, and He will.

So like me, when I was young and unprotected because of my faith issues, many others (proclaimed Christians included) have lost the faith needed to allow God to do what He does, avenge and defend His people. All the enemy needed was a small entry point, and the next thing you know I was confused on what it was I believed. That entry point wasn't so much as because I had given up on God, as it was the fact that I wanted to act on what I felt, more than I was willing to wait on God to correct the problem. I was just like that psalmist asking the Lord "How long will you allow this to go on", but instead of waiting on God like that person, I turned to something else. Many will judge me for that bad decision, but I see it happening at an all-time rate every day. So many believe in a "higher power" now, or they're so called "conscience", or "free thinkers", or that's the white man's religion, or man wrote the bible, or that the black woman is actually god and made man. It's so much out there for an unprotected mind to navigate to, and it's happening all the time. Even a Christian will agree with a social media status that totally contradicts God's word. Liking this, and double tapping that. That "like" is an agreement. Some like, or agree because even though we claim Christianity, like I did when I was younger, they don't know the Word (Mathew 22:29, Hosea 4:6). Others know the Word, but they don't want to wait on God, or should I say lack the faith needed to allow God to operate. That is the same lack of faith that had me in the penitentiary in the first place.

Imagine with me if you will, someone that is a just person, that understands God's purpose in their life, and understand the plight of people (black, white, Spanish, Asian, whoever), or should I say the plight of the world. Someone who didn't get lost in the money, or fame, or just getting a political position. Someone that carried out their purpose and was helping to represent the oppressed while in office. Now let's take your imagination a step further, and lets picture that that someone is some of the young guys that's out here dying and that didn't get a chance because they're being lead to the streets. Because they're being lead like sheep to a slaughter. Imagine the one that was supposed to be the city official was the young guy or young girl that was killed last night, or last week, or last year, or ten years ago. Or they're out here killing themselves on drugs. Or the one doing time, and the reason we love them so is because we know how good of a person they were to everybody. How they took up for everybody, and made sure everybody was straight. The ones that spoke up for people, and didn't allow people to be bullied. They made sure it was a level playing field. Sounds like what I would want in a politician, how about you?

Imagine if I never take my stance in this fight. If I was to let the fact that I have a past tell me what I couldn't do? What if I didn't allow God to use me in ways like writing this book, or making social media statuses that go against everything we were taught in the streets, knowing that the majority of my friends are people from or somehow affected by the street's. Imagine how many others God gave talents that would help with the struggle. What about you? What if you were the one that's supposed to take down a crooked police force, or better the schools in your community? And don't think because you may not be in the right lifestyle that God can't still make that happen. They thought I'd be dead by now.

Again, I ask you what is your purpose in this struggle we complain about? That we blame everybody else but ourselves for not addressing and fixing, when God might have put one of the key ingredients inside of you. Is it a musician, and if so will you mislead, also? Will you mislead in a way that the devil can use you, and no one will be able to recognize because they consider you "real"? Will you talk about the plight of the people like you care, while simultaneously holding them down? Will you talk about how wrong it is to kill our babies, then threaten to kill our babies in the next song, or next verse? Remind you of some of your favorite rappers? Will you be the politician that's more concerned about your bills and stature so you forget what really made you passionate about politics, and what made you get into politics in the first place? Or will you not do your assignment because you don't want to ruffle any feathers?

The great man Moses, in the Bible, was tasked with getting his people free, and leading them to the Promised Land (Exodus 3-40). God had chosen him to do it, and once he got past all of the excuses that he felt made him inadequate to represent God and carry out his purpose, he did what he was supposed to. Of course he ruffled the feathers of the people that had his nation in bondage, but guess who else's feathers got ruffled, his own people. The same people who he was sent to free, and part of the reason was because they were still enslaved mentally. Don't be afraid to ruffle feathers, even if it's the people you are close to or those you are helping (your nation). You were specifically chosen for the task, WHATEVER it may be! That's your purpose!

"Lest Satan should get an advantage of us: for we are not ignorant of his devices."

2 Corinthians 2:11

THE ENTREPRENEUR

Apostle Joseph T. Hackett, a very influential man of our times, in one of his sermons said, "A drug dealer is only an entrepreneur who hasn't found the right product." This statement either implies trickery, bad decision making, or both! Bad decision making for the simple reason that the person chose the wrong investment; it happens every day on Wall Street. Trickery meaning that the person has been deceived into thinking that drugs were the right thing to invest in.

Some of the men and women from my church, as a

part of our outreach ministry (and just because we care), make regular visits to a detention center in Virginia to talk to the youth there. On one visit, while talking to the young guys there, I asked them if they knew that the time, effort, and thought process that it takes to operate in the illegal drug market is the same time, effort, and thought process that a CEO of a company has to put in. Sounds crazy, huh? Well obviously it did to them also, because no one answered. Instead they looked at me for an explanation to my crazy theory. Let's take a look at it. You have to choose the right people to deal with and purchase the product from, whether up front or on consignment, and whether you're going with great product or something less potent for a cheaper price. The person has to choose the right workers, who their target audience will be, where to do business at, how much to invest, how much time it will or should take, have to take note of how much profit of loss was seen, market the product, etc. The list goes on, and we could also go into more elaborate details, but as you can see the two worlds coincide.

The difference in this scenario (or at least one of the main differences besides taxes) is the "cops and robbers." Just like the name of the old game that kids use to play, but different in nature. That's not to say that the people that work don't have to deal with the thought of being robbed, also, but in the streets, that's a common practice.

So, in a sense, a person choosing to run the streets, and make a living illegally, could actually put his or herself through more stress than an honest businessman. That world has a whole different set of penalties, that the other side doesn't have to deal with, or shouldn't have to, but anything can be done in a shady way. The well-known rapper, Jay Z, has a song "D'Evils" (pronounced "da evils", but yeah, as you can see it's spelled devils; his idea of word play), where he said, "Whoever said illegal was the easy way out/Couldn't understand the mechanics, and the workings of the underworld, granted…."

I've rarely come across a person in the streets that wants to do it forever, or that wants to make that their permanent place, and can you guess what their goal is? Yep, to run a legit business. Why not take that same energy that you're using to run that illegitimate business, and put it into whatever it is you really want to do? The enemy has perverted our gift of entrepreneurship and made us feel like the streets are the only way to make those dreams happen. Even if I'm a rapper, I have to hustle, too. Or I have to make street music.

We know the odds are highly in favor of us facing death and /or jail, and most of us have been around long enough to know that's not just something they told us to scare us when we were young. Those really are the odds. We've experienced incarceration ourselves, or seen enough people go, and the same thing goes for the deaths or near death experiences. We have gotten locked up (been incarcerated), came home to try it again, only to get locked back up most of the times. We've been shot or shot at only to come back and try it again. That should be deemed criminal insanity. Why don't we give the right side of life that many chances and/or that much passion that we're willing to die or go to prison for it?

Some will say "this is all we know", and I understand. I understand because I use to agree, when I was warped in that same mindset, but now I see we know so much more. We have different skills that would allow us to succeed if used properly. Those coming up under us have skills and gifts that will allow them to succeed if we pave the way and open some businesses, so that we can offer jobs.

Here's an example: One of the guys I know is serving a life sentence in the federal penitentiary now, and the image that's been painted of him is a monster, a thug; some act like he was the scum of the earth. Dare I say I know him in a totally different way than those images portray? I remember the guy that would give anyone his last, or "the shirt off his back," literally. A young man that was the most adamant against raising the younger guys to think that running the streets was the way to go. A guy that loved to cook, and take care of the people close to him; even those that weren't close to him. What if someone could've gotten to him and shown him the right way, and molded him into making something of his God-given gifts? He probably could've had his own restaurant, mentorship program, or something like a goodwill. Instead, the streets carved out his life, and made an indentation on how he would live. The state of our neighborhoods did to him what it wants to do to everyone else, and the enemy tries to make his grip (or stronghold) in our neighborhoods even tighter.

This is not all we know, it's all we choose to focus on. Though that's not all of our doing, that's the reality, and we have to be willing to change that reality. I'll give you a story I heard once:

There were two twin brothers, raised together in a two-parent household. Their mom tended to the house, their father worked. Their father was an alcoholic who abused the mother in different ways, and the brothers were subject to it growing up. Once they were grown one of the twins also became an alcoholic who abused his wife and lived similar to how his father did. When asked why he lived like that, his response was "Because my father did it." The second twin grew up to never drink nor hit on his wife, when asked why he didn't do it he responded, "Because my father did it." I'm not sure where I heard that story, but the message is clear: The decision is ultimately ours whether we use what we are raised in to make things better or keep the same pattern. Some of our realities are definitely not in our favor, but either we'll use it as an excuse like the first twin, or like the second twin we have to use that as motivation to go the right way. Like some of the people who have come from our same neighborhoods, and same households chose to do. In the story of the twins, that was their reality. One ending is how the enemy hopes it goes, the other is how Christ wants it to be.

Since we're here looking at odds, let's try these: if we don't do something different, our kids will face the same, if not greater odds. If that's not motivation to change, I don't know what is.

WHOSE CHILD ARE YOU?

While we're on the subject of kids, what side of the ledger are you on? Who are you representing? There are only two sides of the coin: good and bad! God and the devil! Jesus, when addressing some of the Jews in John 8:44 (NIV) said, "You belong to your father, the devil, and you want to carry out your father's desires. He was a murderer from the beginning, not holding to the truth, for there is no truth in him. When he lies, he speaks his native language, for he is a liar and the father of lies" In this scripture, Jesus makes it clear that there are definitely people who are children of the devil.

To be even more clear of what's taking place here in the scripture, he was talking to Jews who in a couple of scriptures before that (John 8:41), claimed that they were the children of God. They thought their race/origin/heritage was what made them sons of God. Not everyone that says that they are children of God, or say that they believe in God, or the biggest one "we are all God's children", and any of the other things people say, that makes them sound like they have some form of entitlement to God while they live how they want to, are actually considered to be children of God. The truth of the matter is, whose child we are shows through our ways. 1 John 3:8-10 (NIV) says "The one who does what is sinful is of the devil, because the devil has been sinning from the beginning. The reason the Son of God appeared was to destroy the devil's work. [9] No one who is born of God will continue to sin, because God's seed remains in them; they cannot go on sinning, because they have been born of God. [10] This is how we know who the children of God are and who the children of the devil are: Anyone who does not do what is right is not God's child, nor is anyone who does not love their brother and sister." Righteousness shall show who the children of God are. Living the right way! A lot of scriptures tell us who the children of God are, and how the children of God should operate. John 1:12 says "But as many as received him, to them gave he power to become the sons of God, even to them that believe on his name." When we receive Christ, it shows (manifest) in our righteous living.

With Christ being a major (if not thee) key component, let's take a look and see if we can somehow make a connection as for our lineage, and whether it be of God. Romans 8:29 (NIV) says that "For those God foreknew he also predestined to be conformed to the image of his Son, that he might be the first of many brothers and sisters." Foreknew means to have previous knowledge of; simply put, to "know before". So, God knew us before [now], which lines up with Jeremiah 1:5, "Before I formed thee in the belly I knew thee; and before thou comest forth out of the womb I sanctified thee….", and made it our destiny to be made into the image of His Son, Jesus. So, Jesus was the prototype of how we, his brothers and sisters, should be. Jesus' brothers and sisters, because God, The Father, chose us!

Okay, let's look at it from an different angle, based on something that Jesus spoke of, that gave me a revelation. This may be an unconventional angle, but unconventional might be the best way. The fact that I'm writing this book is unconventional, anyway. Before I go to the scripture, I'll tell you about a conversation I was a part of, via a social media site, that helped confirm the revelation I'm about to share.

One of my younger homeboys had made a post about not snitching, and it went something like "real niggas from around here don't snitch." I wanted to say something, but decided to leave the post alone. I would've left it at that until another one of our homeboys said something similar to what I was thinking. As the comments went on, I tried to steer his thoughts into a different direction, and at one point I even posed the question, "What about being real men?" I asked other things along that path of thought. I went on to quote a verse from a song by Boosie, a well-known rapper, (also featuring the late Pimp C), entitled "Wake UP". Boosie (and Pimp C), in an attempt to steer people away from the streets, list some horrible scenarios and outcomes from living the street life. The verse I quoted was "Convicted all your boys, locked your mama up/Now you gon' turn rat or leave your mama stuck." In response to that my homeboy said something to the extent of "Well ma dukes would be stuck because I'm not breaking the code", implying that if they locked his mother up in an attempt to get him to snitch, then he would leave his mama in jail, who didn't do anything, instead of telling on someone. Then I included his child's mother being arrested, and the possibility of the state taking his child. Though I threw those scenarios in there, my plan was to get him to see that the police would take all of that and more away to get someone to cooperate. I also explained that I wasn't advocating for him to tell on anybody, but to curve his (and anybody else who was reading the post) appetite for the streets. To curb the direction of whoever I could before they are faced with those consequences. I went that far because I couldn't fathom him pushing past the mention of his mother being locked up. Honestly, one of the last things I said in my comments was "I understand, though!" See, no matter how much I wanted him to see what I was saying, I understood where he was coming from, on a couple of levels. I understood from one point, which was the main point he was trying to make: there's absolutely no snitching; that he didn't believe in it, and that he would go to the extreme about it. I understood because me, and others, helped form that way of thinking into his DNA. It's an underlying code where we're from, some of our parents even taught us that. I understood because I'm a team player. I understood because my real dudes are my family.

So, what if I say that he wasn't wrong in the makeup of what he said and what he felt to be right? What if I say that his only fault may have been what side he chose to align himself to and took that stance with? What if I say it wasn't all his fault, or the fault of those like him, that the streets were stealing all of the martyrs? See, my revelation was based off an incident in the scriptures (Luke 8:21) involving Jesus. Jesus was speaking, and while doing so, his mother and brother shows up. Someone interrupted Jesus to tell him that his mother and brother were there. I'm sure that whoever it was that interrupted did it because of who it was, and they felt that his mother and brother were important enough to do so. Jesus' reply though (in Luke 8:21 KJV), was "My mother and brethren are these which hear the word of God, and do it." My revelation came from that exact statement. Jesus considered them family, because of their allegiance to The Father. Could it be the same way for those whom have set their allegiance on the other side? Could it be that when we as teens form brotherhoods and become family out in the streets that it is a principle initiated in the scriptures by Jesus, and we're just tricked into what side of the ledger that bond is formed on? That the devil took what was a pure thing, and perverted it? In the scripture discussed earlier (John 8:44), Jesus said, "...you do the will of your father the devil." If we combine that with the last scripture, if someone does the will of the devil then they are the children (sons) of the devil, and those that combine together with them are brothers, and so they are sons of the devil, also, coming together to do his will.

Yeah, it definitely could be that the concept the

younger homie had of "this is my family," regarding those that are going through the struggle with him, is not a wrong concept at all. According to Jesus, the ones who were going through the struggle with him (or fighting the good fight with him), the ones who weren't his blood brother or blood mother, because of the fact that they chose to stand with him on that, their position transcended that of his natural family. Maybe only in the importance of what was going on at the time, but even if for just a moment, their values/roles/positions switched. Like I said earlier, the only right or wrong is conclusive to which side we choose to make the allegiances on!

JOHN 10:10 PT 1

Jesus, in the first half of the scripture John 10:10 in the bible says, "The thief cometh not, but to steal, and to kill, and to destroy." The comma after "The thief comes not", is to allow us to see, or to put emphasis on what comes next is the only reason that the thief (the devil) comes. That's to steal, and to kill, and to destroy; to do each one individually and simultaneously. If these are the only reasons he comes, then this is his whole agenda. He's trying to accomplish this goal *BY ANY MEANS NECESSARY*!

To accomplish this goal, the devil has to get us off balance by using tactics that won't allow us to recognize it as what he's doing, or that he is the one actually doing it. If he showed up in red with a pitchfork (it is okay to laugh) we would most likely go in a different direction. If he had shown up to Eve as the devil she probably never would've had the conversation, much less eaten the fruit.

The same holds true for your own life. He uses all types of ways to disguise who he really is. Here we'll look at a few of his tactics. Some of his most proven effective forms of deception, and ways he looks to accomplish his goals.

Music

One of the enemy's most prolific ways of reaching and deceiving people is through music. Now, though I've heard it stated that the devil was the head of music in heaven, I won't state it like that since everybody won't be able to see that clearly in scripture. However, what is plain to see is that two major times Lucifer (the devil's name in heaven) is talked about in the bible, there is a clear and distinct correlation with him and music. From the time he was created (Ezekiel 28:13) to the time when he is bought down to the grave (Isaiah 14:11), the association with him and music is evident. So, for someone with such a direct and distinctive connection to music as this, it's safe to say that he knows the value of music. In knowing that value, he understands the power of music, the trajectory of music, and the lulling effect music has altogether.

Music has the power to literally change your mood and/or your course, or even channel your mood. This isn't anything that I have to teach anyone, we all know it from experience. We can feel a certain way, and a song comes on that either has us feeling and thinking a different way, or it enhances how we're already feeling. Or we go looking for songs that fit our mood, or with the intent of changing our mood.

Television and radio have been a way to get a message to the masses for centuries now. Now we have social media, live streaming, and a host of other ways to get what we want out to large quantities of people. Some of the other stuff people do, they probably wouldn't have tried if it wasn't for music, television, or the internet making it acceptable.

Are we still being so naïve that we don't think music has anything to do with the problems that plague our neighborhoods? Now I'm not placing all the blame on music, but let's not kid ourselves. The violence, the drugs, the teen pregnancy, etc. Or is it that we don't care enough to change? We'd rather complain about the killing on social media (that's only if it hits close enough to home), then turn around and to go to the concerts of the same people who promote it. I'll go a step further than promote, and say that they are teaching our kids to be killers.

Is there any other method by which murder, violence, drug selling and things like that are ushered into our neighborhoods? Really think about that question before you answer in disagreement due to your feelings. See, I ask the question because for years I had made excuses for the music I listened to. When we have people who see how we see, and feel how we feel about certain life situations, and can put that into music in the right way, it's truly an art. I made the same excuses "we see the same thing in movies," or "we see the same thing every day." They aren't telling me anything new, or showing me anything that I'm not already accustomed to.

Do these movies really affect us? Not to say that movies and such don't play a part at all, they could give us a liking for guns and for some, a liking or a sense of violence. Looking at a John Stathan movie or a "007" movie or something like that is not really pushing me in that way, though. They don't really intertwine with my spirit. Music on the other hand, that's a whole separate can of worms. Our spirits agree with some of the things that are said, their livelihood, even their complaints.

Now though, I personally have a problem with

anyone who makes complaints about the fact that we need jobs and things, have the means to make jobs, and don't start any. Not only that, but start things like clothing companies, and because it's better on their pockets, the clothing manufacturing companies are in another country, while we do everything under the sun to obtain it. Also, I've seen different people post comments on social media about how much money churches (mainly African American churches) have taken in over time, and in those same posts, falsely accuse all these churches (because they group them all together) of not doing anything. Yet the same people making the post will have a favorite rapper or singer make more in one night, or on one tour, than what some of these churches make in a year. Musicians make this amount of money while still making songs calling our sisters, daughters, and whoever else all sorts of derogatory words, at the same time teaching them how to gyrate and move in sensual ways, and people won't have a problem with that. No complaints at all.

Will listening to these things help us deal with the things they are talking about? Are they helping me cope with it? How about helping me with a strategy to get out of the situation. If someone is talking about something positive, we look at them like they're whack. That's immaturity on our parts! Then we don't have any filter on what we let our kids listen to. Or we have a semi filter on it. The "I better not catch you listening to this, but if comes on while we're together it's cool" filter. In that way, we send our kids a lot of mixed signals. Then when they imitate what they hear, and in many cases already see, we want to get mad and beat them. We teach kids how to do wrong so much it's crazy. We teach them how to be sneaky, how to be doubleminded, and not take a solid stance on things, or we teach them not to have any morals at all, and as I said earlier, they get punished for it. That's the same thing crooked cops do. We know it's wrong when they do it, but not for ourselves. You saying "I'm grown" is just like them saying "I'm the police".

Let's look at the drugs people are taking. We can start with something newer like "Molly", or a drug a little older like "X". Now clearly I can't say that these drugs wouldn't have spread at all, but do you think the impact would've been as effective and as sudden without music cosigning for them? "Molly" was a scary drug at first so people were leaving it alone, then some rappers start talking about it, and it becomes cool enough to take a chance on.

Older drugs like "Syrup" (or lean, or whatever they call it where you're from) have been around forever. Still, the effect of music has made it even more popular. So, now everyone has to have some mixed in their cup or their soda bottle. I don't even want to get into pills.

I remember seeing videos of people who had taken bath salts, and how they had lost control. I've also seen gruesome videos of a newer drug, "Crocodile," that rots people's limbs from the inside. I wonder if a rapper starts talking about crocodile like it's cool or like it's the best thing out there right now, would people go out there and start using it. Sad to say, but based on our track record, the answer is yes.

We can listen to a rapper say something like "The game ain't dead/these niggas just scared." Now we know that by "game" he is referring to the "drug game." Well, let's take a look and see; let's check out his theory.

According to Northern Iowa federal district judge, Mark Bennett, in a piece written in "The Nation," he states: "Never could I have imagined that…..after nineteen years [as a federal district court judge], I would've sent 1,092 of my fellow citizens to prison for mandatory minimum sentences ranging from sixty months to life without the possibility of release. The majority of these women, men and young adults are nonviolent drug addicts." What about the kingpins? "I can count them on one hand…."!

In another section, he says, "If lengthy mandatory minimums for nonviolent drug addicts actually worked, one might be able to rationalize them. But there is no evidence that they do. I have seen how they leave hundreds of thousands of young children parentless and thousands of aging infirm and dying parents childless. They destroy families and mightily fuel the cycle of poverty and addiction."

As we can tell by what this federal judge is saying, something is dead, and steadily dying. We make the decision on whether it'll be the "game", or continue to be us (and our kids and parents) for trying to keep the "game" alive.

> You still shooting up Youtube
> You still rapping bout the guns got
> You still rapping about cooking crack
> You still rapping bout the trap
> Man listen I aint trying to judge people
> But all that stuff is destroying people....
> "New Thangs", by Artist Anderson

SUBSTANCES

Well, since we're basically already on the subject of drugs…. how do we fight off the attacks if we're too out of our mind to see what's going on? 1 Peter 5:8 (NIV), "Be alert and of sober mind. Your enemy the devil prowls around like a roaring lion looking for someone to devour." Your enemy the devil. Your adversary the devil. Is looking to devour you i.e. to kill, and to steal, and destroy you. This scripture, from over 2,000 years ago, out of the book that they want you to believe is fake, is warning you of something very relevant today, and is advising us to be sober and watchful for it. Do you think it's a coincidence that marijuana is being legalized? Or that everyone thinks drinking is okay? I didn't speak much on it earlier, but look at how the pill epidemic has taken over. This is not by happenchance, it's a carefully plotted attack on who you are, and who you were created to be. The more out of your right element you are, the easier it is to lay the trap. The more addictions, or the stronger the drug the harder it is for us to come back off. Proverbs 31:4-5, "It is not for kings, O Lemuel, it is not for kings to drink wine; nor for prince's strong drink: Lest they drink and forget the law, and pervert the judgement of any of the afflicted."

Most of the time drinking/drugging is combined with partying. Everything is a party. How many kids suffer from lack of attention, because their parents find it more appealing to be out partying? How many college funds have we smoked up, drank up, or left at the club? Don't think I'm being judgmental, because believe me, I could've sent a couple kids to Harvard for their masters.

Even if we don't like to party, using different substances takes away from who we are. Drugs change the way our body operates, either mentally or physically, or both. Our bodies (and our being) are being hijacked, and we're assisting in the process. This also leads back to who's doing the hijacking? Would God want you out of sorts on some substance that makes you different than the way He made you? Of course not; a baby can answer that question. We can see that from the scriptures above (Proverbs 31:4-5, 1 Peter 5:8). He wants you sober and alert; that scripture is a warning. He has given you all the mental capacity that you need to handle whatever life has for you; whatever life throws your way. The funny thing is the trick is so evident, no drug has ever made a problem go away, not for me. It doesn't even give us the freedom of not thinking about it. For me, whenever I was high and/or drunk (inebriated), I thought more on whatever situation(s) that I was dealing with at the time, and maybe even added some to it.

In fact, let's take a look at the one drug that is supposed to be harmless (and most people agree even though they know it's not). They call it the gateway drug like it's not a drug. The un-addictive drug that the nation is legalizing. Yeah, you guessed it—good ol' marijuana! Better known as "weed," and a hundred other names. In an article titled "Marijuana: Myths & Facts, The 'Truth Behind 10 Popular Misconceptions'", by the Office of Drug Control Policy, in an attempt to do away with the falsehoods associated with the drug, the author writes:

> Marijuana is the most widely used illicit drug in the United States. According to the National

Survey on Drug Use and Health (formerly called the National Household Survey on Drug Abuse), 95 million Americans age 12 and older have tried "pot" at least once, and three out of every four illicit drug users reported using marijuana within the previous 30 days. Use of marijuana has adverse health, safety, social, academic, economic, and behavioral consequences. And yet, astonishingly, many people view the drug as "harmless". The widespread perception of marijuana as a benign natural herb seriously detracts from the most basic message our society needs to deliver: It is not OK for anyone - especially young people – to use this or any other illicit drug.

I don't know about you, but that doesn't seem harmless to me. In fact, the sentence about the consequences is scary. It says *adverse health, safety, social, academic,* and *behavioral* consequences. *Adverse* means preventing success or development; harmful; unfavorable. So, weed prevents success or development and is harmful to all of those critical areas of life. Vital areas of life, and when you pair that with the fact that people are starting at 12 (and even earlier) according to the article, we're stunting development at the most developmental time.

In the article, the ten myths that the writer is

discussing is his/her Table of Contents. In the section about the so-called harmlessness of the drug the writer states:

> Marijuana harms in many ways, and kids are the most vulnerable to its damaging effects. Use of the drug can lead to significant health, safety, social, and learning or behavioral problems, especially for young users. Making matters worse is the fact that the marijuana available today is more potent than ever. Short term effects of marijuana use include memory loss, distorted perception, trouble with thinking and problem solving, and anxiety. Students who use marijuana may find it hard to learn, thus jeopardizing their ability to achieve their full potential.

The writer then goes on to list and explain some of the ways that the drug is harmful. Some of those things were cognitive impairment, mental health, and long term consequences. Let's take a quick look at the first two:

Cognitive Impairment

Cognitive – of, relating to, or involving conscious mental activities (such as thinking, understanding, learning, and remembering). Impair – to make weaker or worse. Some of the things listed in this section of the article that marijuana effects are concentration, thinking attention, memory, sensory, time perception, and coordinated movement. Who needs any of those things, though, right? The article also stated, "Another study, conducted at the University of Iowa College of Medicine, found that people who used marijuana frequently (7 or more times weekly for an extended period of time) showed deficits in mathematical skills and verbal expression, as well as selective impairments in memory retrieval processes."

Mental Health

The writer begins to describe how the drug is harmful to the brain by describing the use of marijuana in comparison to the [perceived] harder drugs.

> Smoking marijuana leads to changes in the brain similar to those caused by cocaine, heroin, and alcohol. All of these drugs disrupt the flow of chemical neurotransmitters, and all have specific receptor sites in the brain that have been linked to feelings of pleasure and, over time addiction.

What's amazing to me is, in order to pass some of the laws that are floating around right now regarding marijuana, their first goal is to trick (or sell a dummy to) the public so they are thinking the drug isn't addictive.

This article, from a governmental agency, clearly tells us the drug has the same addictive components as cocaine and heroin. That's nothing they had to tell me. I see whole neighborhoods addicted to it. Whole genre's and generations addicted to it. I see people who have been using it for 20 plus years. I myself was addicted to it for 20 plus years. I'm here to point out the dummy that's being sold to us, the rest is up to you. But we can't go along with the dummy just because we want to benefit off of it, just because we want to continue smoking. Pretty soon, it will be our daughter out there smoking. It'll be our 12-year-old son out there smoking weed, cutting short his potential. It'll be your son that makes it to the NFL that everybody is judging, calling him sad or dumb or stupid, because he's getting ready to lose a multi-million dollar deal because he can't stop smoking weed… or can't stop popping pills and drinking.

CIRCUMSTANCES

Another way is our situations, or circumstances. Most notably poverty and the likes of it. Now, first of all, it's hard to lay blame in these types of situations. Some people come from harsh, dire living arrangements where day to day living is catastrophic. I'm talking middle of the worst neighborhoods, dad is gone, mom is getting high and/or drunk, house is cold, nobody is doing anything, and "I have to eat" situations. If you jump out there as a young kid because you and/or your siblings have to eat, it's hard for a man to say that you're wrong. Though, the reality of things is, you are wrong. I'd be lying to say that I don't understand, but I would be equally as wrong to not give you the truth. To go deeper into that (because I know it will be a hard pill for some to swallow), just say you go out to sell drugs because that's your situation. If we sell drugs to better our situation, won't that put someone (mainly in your own neighborhood) in the same predicament? Another thing is, we start determining what's bad enough. So, if I feel like I'm living in dire circumstances, which might be luxury to the next person, it's time to hustle or do something illegal.

What I'm saying is not all of us have that same testimony or story. Not even some of us that came up in those same bad neighborhoods, because truth be told, though we came up there, we had it fairly better than some of the others. Our parents did what they could, whether it was single parents (like most of our stories are) or both. I won't act like the reality of everyday life and surviving in these neighborhoods isn't enough to be a just cause in some people's thought pattern, but we can't do wrong to make things right. We learned that way back in elementary school when we were being taught about "Robin Hood" and his merry band of thieves. That was the moral of that childhood tale. So, whether we're the kid with absolutely nothing going right, or suffering from being from places where nothing right seems to come our way, we still have to seek the right way to do things.

That's where a solid belief in God comes into play. We are not the only ones who have had to miss meals, and as bad as it sounds, the reality of it is we won't be the last. Those before us made it, some amongst us made it, and there will be some after us to make it without doing wrong. For those that don't make it, the question becomes why not? Will it be because of us not living a productive enough life to change the pattern of their lives? Will it be because we didn't even try the right way? We say we hustle to feed our kids, but when we're taken away due to incarceration or death, the situation or circumstance becomes much worse. All of these things leave them to fend for themselves and have to make the same detrimental decisions on choosing what the devil is offering over the promises of God.

I know many will disagree with what I'm saying, and I understand that. Do something for me first, though. Go talk to a mother (or any family member, or friend; loved one) of someone lost to the streets, whether death or incarceration, and ask would they have rather missed a few more meals, or went without some things a little while longer, instead of having their loved one try the streets.

I reiterate, we cannot do wrong to make things right.

That goes for the violence as well. Again, if the Lord says vengeance is His in Romans 12:19, then we can't take vengeance into our own hands, and say we're believing God. We can't continue killing each other. Even if someone kills someone we know. Not even someone we care about. Now, I know that's going to be almost impossible for most to accept, and people won't agree with that statement, even though we know what the word of God says. The thing is if we take these types of issues into our own hands, we take God out of the equation, and put ourselves in God's place. We void the scripture. Why else would God have to say "Vengeance is Mine" unless He knew there would be cases that would drive us to the point of seeking vengeance on our own? At that point though, He wants us to allow Him to handle it.

We have to trust God, it's mandatory, it's essential! Trusting God means we have to do so not only in the best times, but mainly in the worst. The Bible references people in terrible situations. Whether it was the Israelites in captivity in Egypt (Exodus 1-13), or Job's story (Job), or Daniel in the lion's den (Daniel 6), or David fighting Goliath (1 Samuel 17), and many other stories in the Bible (almost the whole book) that are there for you to see that the promises of God will prevail, always!

On the flip side of that is the curses, and they are also concrete. Even when we feel that we have acted justly, the repercussions remain. Two of Jacob's sons, Simeon and Levi, killed to avenge the rape of their sister, Dinah in Genesis 34. Most of us would give a stamp of approval for an act like that. A lot of people will understand. Yet, in Genesis 49, when Jacob is blessing some of his sons before his death, what Simeon and Levi received could be viewed more as curses. Genesis 49:5-7 (NIV), "Simeon and Levi are brothers—their swords are weapons of violence. 6Let me not enter their council, let me not join their assembly, for they have killed men in their anger and hamstrung oxen as they pleased. 7Cursed be their anger, so fierce, and their fury, so cruel! I will scatter them in Jacob and disperse them in Israel."

Greed

We know that everyone that chooses the streets doesn't do it from being bad off (coming from rough environments), or because "there's no other way." Then one of the main reasons that cause people to do it has to be addressed, which is greed. "But those who desire to be rich fall into temptation, into a snare, into many senseless and harmful desires that plunge people into ruin and destruction" (1 Timothy 6:9). Can you imagine if we didn't take everything the enemy gave us and then blame the ruin and destruction on someone else? Let me give an example: Somehow on these social media sites, a picture and narrative of what is said to be Black Wall Street, periodically pops up. I understand what people are trying to get out, but my thought is "How did they do that?" What I'm saying is, if they did that during those times, why can't we do it now? I refuse to believe that times are worse for us now. The greed doesn't allow us to see past the nose on our face, though. We want some money now. We are not lining up to go to college, most don't even have the desire to, but the streets are packed. Nobody is trying to start a business without resulting to drugs first.

There are many other ways, also. So, whether it's music, circumstances, greed, or any of the other factors not mentioned, the plan is to keep us focused on those areas we see with our carnal eye. Or focused on our desires so that they lead us astray (James 1:14). So, how many dreams have to be killed, and how many families have to be destroyed before we see that this is clearly the devil? Now if you mix the **music**, with the **drugs**, with the **circumstances**.... Well that's almost like a witch's brew. Don't fall for the trick Hansel and Gretel, and end up in the oven. (John 15:6) "If you do not remain in me, you are like a branch that is thrown away and withers; such branches are picked up, thrown into the fire and burned."

STEWART BROCKENBROUGH

RIGHT OR WRONG

"I got your back, whether right or wrong" is a relatable statement or feeling of mostly everybody living. It symbolizes a level of loyalty. It says that no matter the circumstances, "I'm here for you", "I support you." Even when you're wrong, you're right, and I'm rolling with you. In some instances, we feel like it's the right way to be. Husband and wife, family, commander and army, king and kingdom are all instances where we would deem that statement to hold true.

Is there a point when that form of loyalty is not the

"right" thing to do even when the bonds that were mentioned before are in play? What if it goes against your morals? Al Pacino, in his role as Tony Montana in the well-known movie "Scarface," was sent with a group of guys on a mission by his boss to carry out a murder that was much needed. An unexpected twist occurred when the guy happened to be riding with his wife and kids. Tony, who had no problem with killing, (he had carried out a contract earlier in the movie), didn't believe in the killing of women or children. The guy he was with knew that this "hit" had to be carried out, or they would be held responsible, and probably killed if it isn't done, so he wasn't fazed by the intended target's family riding with him. Tony warned him "no wife no kids," but this has to happen. Tony ends up killing the guy he's with before he is able to carry out the hit of killing the assigned guy and his family. It was something Tony didn't believe in. Even though it would seem right, on the wrong side of things, to have gone along with the order, his morals meant more. That's just a movie though, right?

Well, in Chicago, they baited a little boy into the alley and killed him because of a supposed problem they had with his father. They shot the little boy several times. He died in his school uniform with the basketball he kept with him just a few feet from his body. This is how it was described in a CNN report from the arrest of his alleged murderer some four weeks later:

An autopsy of Tyshawn's body showed two perforating gunshot wounds, and part of his right thumb was lost as a defensive wound trying to block a gunshot, court papers said. The boy's body had a gunshot wound to the head, a bullet graze wound to his right upper back, and a superficial wound to the right forearm, documents said. "There was evidence of close-range firing," court papers said.

Makes my blood boil just thinking about it, and if this doesn't affect you in the same way, then there's something wrong with you! The suspect's brother had gotten killed in a car while with his mother. The mother was also wounded. Disturbing things like this happen on the regular all across this country, and very few people are doing anything about it. See, it is suspected that several people were present when that little boy was murdered. I wonder if one of them could've changed the outcome of that day.

What will you do to help the outcome? We have to protect the kids from these horrendous acts. Think about how this will affect all the kids from Tyshawn's area, all the kids in his family. What are we going to do, just vote, or just get guns? Are guns going to help the issue or hurt it? How will you save your family? I'm going to save mines! The generational curse stops here. My last name has been associated with crime in my city for forever it seems. I do this so it won't have to be like that for the generation's coming up behind me. I'm going to make sure I'm attached to the kingdom of God, first, because God chose me. Then in doing so, I will attach our name to all the blessings that God has for us. Books, businesses, music, whatever.

"All things are possible through God who strengthens us."

In order to do so, we can't be afraid to go against the grain. For some it's not an option, anyway. Life will force you to see that you're totally different than your situation and bigger than your circumstances. You're not going to fit in no matter what you do. You will always have that pull, or inner feeling that there is more to you, and it won't always be because you're down bad. Just look at Moses. He had it made, raised in the Pharaoh's home, bought up with the Pharaoh's kids, and still there was a pull that let him know that there was something else that he was supposed to be doing. Some of you have that pull to do something different, also. That pull will not only save you, but your family and the other people close to you.

The second chapter of Joshua in the Bible tells the story of Rahab and her courageous but daring protection and evacuation of some spies which lead to the rescue and evacuation of her loved ones. Joshua, Israel's appointed leader after the death of Moses, sends two spies out into the lands that they are getting ready to occupy, with emphasis on the city of Jericho. Once there, they encounter one of the towns own, Rahab, a prostitute. Rahab gave the spies a place to stay for the night. While they were there, the king of Jericho was informed that there were some spies in the land, and that they were at Rahab's house. The king sent word for Rahab to send out the spies. Instead of obeying the king and sending them out, she hid them. Then she came up with a story about how the spies had been there, but they had left before the gates to the city had closed.

She also told the guards the king had sent that if they gave pursuit they could probably catch the spies. When the guards went in search of the spies, she went back to the spies and told them how the people of the land were all scared, even the men. After making them swear an oath that they would spare her and her family when they came back to take the land, and receiving keen instructions from the spies on what to do and how it would happen, she let them out the window and down the wall with a red chord. When the Israelites came back to take the land, they of course held true to their word, and her and her family were saved. Not only that, but she was considered justified (James 2:25).

See, what had the people of the town so scared is that they had heard of what God was doing for the Israelites. They had already heard of how He was definitely with them, causing the Israelites to be successful in war, and they knew that the Israelites were coming their way. So, instead of just going along with it, Rahab did something. It was similar to what people who change their lives over have to do, which is not follow the pack; not allow the darkness to lead them.

Rahab, a prostitute, sinner, heathen, and whatever else you want to call her, went against the grain and saved her family from sure destruction. She could've went along with the flow, and allowed herself, along with her family, to face the same destruction the people of the land were sure to face, because they couldn't break away from the norm. Be it fear, family ties, comfortability, or whatever, we have to be the ones willing to make the change.

Are you willing to be the one that makes it? Like really, or are you okay with living and believing the lie that's being told, or should I say sold to you? I know that's not your desire, and I know that through experience. Though we come to grips with it being a possibility, and some even accept it as a likelihood, nobody wants to die in the streets! That's one of the main reasons we take chances of getting locked up with guns. I never wanted to die in the streets, I never felt like that was my purpose.

Nevertheless, I made myself come to grips with the fact that it was a strong possibility that it could happen. Whether I felt like that was my ultimate demise or not, it doesn't change the fact that it was the devils ultimate plan for me. It was what he desired for me, and for everyone else living that life. "To kill, and to steal, and to destroy." We know that's his only aim, so why continue to be naïve, when we know we want nothing more than to live?

I've seen so many of the younger guys mature because of the fact that they have become fathers. I know that they desire to be in their kid's lives and to watch them grow. The enemy will use that against you, if given the chance. What do you think was the determining factors in a lot of people's lives that made them get on the stand? You don't think that seeing their kids grow was a part of that? No, I'm not here to condone any one thing or another, and I'm not calling the government the enemy. The devil knows how much of a clutch the demonic system of snitching is on us, and the way people are looked at about it. It's enforced by fear! You see earlier my homeboy said if it's snitching or his mother, his mother had to go. You don't think the enemy has his hand in a mindset like that? Come on family! I'm here on assignment from God, and I have an understanding of how things go. "No snitching" sounds good and all until it's your people, and you need the answers, then it's a different story.

Recently a very young girl was shot in Richmond (VA), and I watched as the town cried out for someone to come forward. If that's the case, then we have to watch how we implicate these "demonic systems". Yeah, "no snitching" is a systematic structure. It's a way to keep doing wrong. We have to watch what we hand down to the youth. They'll hear "no snitching", watch someone raped and killed and not want to come forth. If anyone thinks that that's cool, imagine if it's your daughter, sister, mother, aunt, or grandmother that it happens to. Then we want someone to come forth and break the same code that we have enforced, even if we have the wrong intentions about the justice that's to be issued out.

Again, although we have some wise kids, they don't comprehend things on the same level. Not only that, but when people receive things before they are ready, whether kid or adult, that's detrimental. When the kids are trying to do things that they see or hear, it's up to them how they will imitate life. When they're given things to deal with too early, 9 times out of 10 they won't get it right without some kind of guidance. Whether that's them imitating what they see and hear, or just a life situation. We can't keep going down the same roads that those before us traveled, then we've traveled, seen it wasn't good, then still depict it like it's cool to those coming up behind us. They take that same imagery that we burn into their heads and take off with it in any way they want. That's what I call the "trickle-down effect," when we pass these things down then expect the kids to get it right. It happens a lot in our communities, especially in the streets.

That's one of the reasons I've always been against charging or trying kids as adults. Their minds aren't fully developed and therefore aren't fully comprehending what's taking place, even if their minds are fully comprehending what's taking place (yeah, you read that right). Their comprehension levels are not up to par, which is why they are considered youth in the first place, right? Give a 10-year-old and a thirty year old the same situation, and the length of life alone will be a direct cause of the different comprehensions.

That's not to say that the 10-year-old didn't fully comprehend, in their own way, what was going on. It's evident that comprehension changes as we grow. An example of that is me not viewing the streets the same as I did as a teenager, and many other clear examples as to why comprehension is directly related and associated with growth. How, as a young person we do things for fun at times, and because we don't fully "get" what the consequences are, and how much they would affect our lives. Ask anyone who is affected by a felony from making childish moves, or who feels they had kids too early, or anything they would've done differently. Not just because of how it turned out for them then, but because had they been a little older and wiser they never would've made some of those choices in the first place. 1 Corinthians 13:11, "When I was a child, I talked like a child, I thought like a child, I reasoned like a child. When I became a man, I put the ways of childhood behind me." No one should be tried as an adult if they haven't been given the proper time to grow and mature. I don't care if their eighteenth birthday is the next day. They are not able to buy tobacco or alcohol, but we can send them to maximum security prison with grown men, sometimes for the rest of their lives. In Pennsylvania, there's about 500 children automatically sentenced to life without parole who have to be resentenced because the United States Supreme Court struck down automatic life-without-parole sentences for children in Miller v Alabama in 2012. In light of this ruling, many states have abolished the life-without-parole sentences for juveniles. Philadelphia District Attorney Seth Williams, when talking with reporters, told them he wouldn't be seeking new life-without-parole sentences. He told the Philadelphia Inquirer, "It's my goal to give all of these individuals some light at the end of the tunnel."

    I don't want to keep blaming the system for everything, and that's not because I don't feel like it's a major part of the problem. Proverbs 29:2 "When the godly are in authority, the people rejoice. But when the wicked are in power, they groan." I'm also not here to act like people are wrong for how they feel about the government. We have constant reminders that the justice system is out of order, and at times makes no common sense. I don't want to blame them when the teens are tried as adults when we know this is happening and we allow them to face that fate by not correcting some of their ways before it even gets to that point. I don't want to blame the system when in fact, we aren't showing the teens a better way. We coax our younger cousins into the same ignorance that we've lived and died in for so long. We think just telling them it's wrong is going to deter them. Nah, we know that's bogus because it didn't deter any of us. In some cases, no matter how much effort we put out, it probably won't make a difference, but they at least need to see that everybody doesn't just agree with any and everything.

They need to see some people take a stand. They need some more mothers like the one that caught her son out trying to be a part of the Baltimore riots, and went off on him. We need some men with that same aggression. Men that are willing to go hard about leading the youth in the right direction. Some men like Keynon Lake and the MDTMT (My Daddy Taught Me That) foundation out of Asheville NC, and many others around the nation who are actively stepping in and affecting the lives of young males.

It's from the false imagery that we present that we cause them to believe in falsehoods, because a lot of them look(ed) up to us out in the streets. No matter where you're from, it's something about the street in the generation before you that attracted you to it. Maybe it was the lifestyle all together, or maybe it was just the money, the women, how they were respected or feared, or that they could offer protection. Maybe it was from a noble and pure place in your mind (the Robin Hood effect), like supporting an impoverished family, and/or being able to look out for the neighborhood. Whatever it may be from that generation, it helped usher you into your infatuation for that side of life.

If they never see anyone do it right, then we affect whether they believe it can be done or not. We affect whether they feel they have to sell drugs or play ball as the only two options for making it out of the hood. It would be great if they could be able to say my dad, or my uncle, or my aunt, mother, or Mr. or Ms. So-and-So down the street made it and did it the right way, and so can I. The more numbers we have on the side of the people doing it the right way, the better our chances of saving our youth, and producing positive and productive individuals.

Instead, we've been praising the people that do wrong. We hold high regards for the things that are done out of the wrong content. WE BRAG ABOUT THE HIGHEST MURDER RATE. We brag about the worst neighborhoods, and gangs or groups. Women are attracted to knuckleheads or "Mr. Wrongs" (and vice versa), and so on.

The different demonic systems are set in place for us to stay on the wrong side, to keep us trapped in while we think it's keeping us free. Another dummy we've bought. It's killing us, stealing us, and it's destroying us, and we're cool with it. We can't see it because we're trapped on that side. Galatians 4:3, "Even so we, when we were children, were in bondage under the elements of the world."

The question is how do we win? How do we break away from the norm and obtain real freedom? Well first we must understand that real freedom is not a flesh thing, it's spiritual. Sometimes we take something that's naturally spiritual, and make it about your flesh. We serve gods based upon what makes us feel good. 2 Timothy 4:3-4, "For a time is coming when people will no longer listen to sound and wholesome teaching. They will follow their own desires and will look for teachers who will tell them whatever their itching ears want to hear. They will reject the truth and chase after myths." Everything about God won't feel good, but it will feel good. What I mean is, we're human, and we will go through life like other humans. With that being said, we will be affected the same way. Pain will hurt, death will make us grieve, there will be joyous times, mistakes will cost us, we will face temptations, and so on. It's not like the Bible is a golden wand, and we are now exempt from those things. When I say we feel good, it's because of our understanding that God is in control. Whatever we are going through, it's for the greater good, even in the struggle.

Spiritual freedom is releasing the weight. It's acknowledgement that something greater is in control. Something greater than man is directly connected to who I am, and what makes me. That something greater is God. Romans 5:3-5 (KJV) says, "And not only so, but we glory in tribulation also: knowing that tribulation worketh patience; And patience, experience; and experience, hope: And hope maketh not ashamed; because the love of God is shed abroad in our hearts by the Holy Ghost which is given unto us." We know that there's something way bigger going on even when the things seem out of whack. That's where our faith supersedes life. That's a part of where freedom lies for us. 2 Corinthians 3:17 (KJV), "Now the Lord is the Spirit, and where the Spirit of the Lord is, there is freedom."

There's only one God, and just because everybody says that, that doesn't put them in agreement with us.

James 2:19 (NLT), "You say you have faith, for you believe that there is one God. Good for you! Even the demons believe this, and they tremble in terror." I say this because other religions will lean on the fact that they believe in one god, also. The difference is Jesus, and the fact that he is the Son. John 14:6-7 (NIV), "Jesus answered, "I am the way and the truth and the life. No one comes to the Father except through me. 7 If you really know me, you will know my Father as well. From now on, you do know him and have seen him."

If we don't obtain spiritual freedom, then it doesn't matter where we are or what we get, we'll still be in bondage and chains. People who are spiritually free can be incarcerated and experience freedom, while people on the outside are enslaved. Doesn't matter what side of the fence you're on, if you're spiritually enslaved then you're a captive.

I feel like I always had buck, or some kind of noncompliance in me, because of injustice, or because I determined what laws I was supposed to serve under. Whether I ran the streets or not, I held doors for people, I respected my elders, etc. I know others that do the same. We know right—it's in us. (Romans 2:14, "For when the Gentiles, which have not the law, do by nature the things contained in the law, these having not the law, are a law unto themselves." The Gentiles were, among other things, the unlearned as it related to the laws of God. One of the things this scripture is speaking on is how people know by nature what's right and wrong.) Others have that same buck in them! It has to sit right with our spirit. Anything outside of that doesn't sit well with us, and we're not rocking with it. The thing is, if we're not spiritually inclined, it will be hard for us to determine the difference between what's just feelings, and what's truly our spirit speaking to us.

Like I talked about earlier, Moses had it good. He was raised in the Pharaoh's palace, with the Pharaoh's kids. He had the best food, best teachings, the best of everything, yet he knew injustice. He knew what wasn't right, and it was something he could not ignore. No matter how comfortable he was physically, he was uncomfortable spiritually. His discomfort was directly connected to his purpose. It led him to murder, but that wasn't the way that God wanted it done. That was man's way! That was a move in his feelings that was going to get him tried, and probably executed. He knew that he was supposed to do something (Acts 7:25 (NIV) "Moses thought that his own people would realize that God was using him to rescue them, but they did not."). The thing is doing it the right way. Romans 12:21(NIV) says, "Do not be overcome by evil, but overcome evil with good." When he went back with God backing him (or leading him), he didn't have to lay a finger on anyone.

Freedom is found in Christ! We have to cherish that freedom. Freedom is salvation, which is offered through and by Jesus Christ. Once this freedom is found, we are to cherish and hold on to it. The word of God tells us:

Roman 8:32 (ESV) "There is therefore now no condemnation for those who are in Christ Jesus. For the law of the Spirit of life has set you free in Christ Jesus from the law of sin and death….."

Galatians 5:1 (KJV) "Stand fast therefore in the liberty wherewith Christ hath made us free, and be not entangled again with the yoke of bondage."

John 8:32 (NLT) "And you will know the truth, and the truth will set you free."

John 8:36 (NLT) "So if the Son sets you free, you are truly free."

Romans 8:21 (ESV) "That the creation itself will be set free from its bondage to corruption and obtain the freedom of the glory of the children of God."

Galatians 5:13 (ESV) "For you were called to freedom, brothers. Only do not use your freedom as an opportunity for the flesh, but through love serve one another."

WHAT AM I PROMISED?

Hosea 4:6 (KJV), in the Bible says, "My people are destroyed for lack of knowledge: because thou hast rejected knowledge, I will also reject thee, that thou shalt be no priest to me: seeing thou hast forgotten the law of thy God, I will also forget thy children." We are being destroyed (in all ways) from our lack of knowledge (awareness of). This is notoriously true when it comes to the promises of God, and with that being the case it gives way to a lot of things that are allowing it to look like the enemy is winning.

If you don't know what's going on, you become susceptible to situations of all sorts. They call it being "blindsided." (So, it's funny when people are so called "conscience" now, in the sense that they have found something greater, outside of God. How about getting "conscience" of God, the Creator of all things?) We're being blindsided when the information is right in front of us. The promises of God are right in that book that sits in everyone's home collecting dust, as if having the book in our house will make it magically work.

In the movie "The Book of Eli," the main character, played by Denzel Washington, was able to do all that he did, and able to endure all that he did for two reasons: 1) He had the book (The Word) in him. 2) He believed [in] it. You know what's even crazier, his enemy knew the power of that same word, and knew (believed) what he could do with that book. The difference was the intentions. That should be the difference between you and Satan. That should be the difference between you and those that read the book only to use it against those who believe in the goodness of it. It shouldn't be the fact that you don't even know what's going on, like the rest of the people in the movie, just thumbing along to whatever was happening.

The enemy (Satan) knows what the word can do, he

was in heaven with God. He believes in the power of The Word. The enemy was there when God formed the Earth; when God said let there be light, and we're still witnessing that light today.

How can you expect to receive something if you don't even know that it's promised, and if you do receive it, how will you recognize it? That's the thing, you can't. You can receive something that looks good, call it a blessing, and it would be the total opposite. In other words tricked, or "sold a dummy." Don't believe me, ask someone who has been in a relationship with someone they thought was God sent, and that person was in fact a distraction used by the enemy. If you don't even know it's promised, then maybe you're going out of your way, maybe even breaking laws, to receive something that God already has planned for you anyway, if you just go the right way (or "The Way" John 14:6). To know the right way to go about things, knowing the Word is essential. Without it, it's automatic destruction! That's where belief kicks in. If you believe [in God], like most of us say we do, then you take heed to what's being said in the scripture Hosea 4:6, you see the value of "knowing."

The musical artist Mali Music has a song called "Royalty." In the song, he asks questions of both the male and female population:

"Would you give them everything/ would you let them

call you those names if you knew you were a queen?/ And my brother would you be out here risking your life for green paper/if you knew you had it all already/if you knew you were a king?"

If you knew, would you still be doing what it is you're doing? More than likely not. I'm not talking the "God is good" and "God will make a way" cliché sayings, though they are very true. I'm talking about knowing why God is good, and how He will make a way or has already made a way.

I see a lot of people that want to make a difference, that want to do "something" to help themselves, their families, or just to help the cause, altogether. That's great, because like me, you were wired to do so, you were wired to pursue what's right. The thing is, how do we do it without knowing what to do? In the Bible it's called a zeal without knowledge (Romans 10:1-3), wanting to do the right thing, but not knowing what the right thing is, nor the right way to go about it.

An example of that is every time we get puffed up about something we want to go to war, but war is not the answer to everything, believe me. Without knowing the right way to do things, we can mislead people, and depending on your influence it will determine how many people you mislead. We all know that that's called "the blind leading the blind." Hear me when I speak, because I see a lot of things going on in the world, especially on social media. People sound really good, and very intelligent. They are so misleading, and a lot of people navigate to it, a lot of times because of the racial uplifting/downgrading that's attached to the message. A lot of memes that have a seemingly godly nature to it, but isn't Godly at all. Some of the main people agreeing with the ignorance are "Christian." Not only agreeing with it, but spreading it (by reposting and sharing it). Sharing it with other people who think it's right, because they are unaware that it's all wrong. They agree with it because it sounds right and feels good. I'm not nitpicking (I can't nitpick on something I'm guilty of myself), I'm just pointing things out so that we are aware of how important it is to know what is and what is not right.

Proverbs 19:2 (KJV) tells us, "Also, that the soul be without knowledge, it is not good; and he that hasteth with his feet sinneth." This scripture says that to be without knowledge is not good for you, and it's wrong to rush into things without knowledge, or to move hastily (hurried) before knowing the matter. Or to be in the "Fastlane" not knowing that God already desires for you to live a wonderful life; if we choose to go about it the right (righteous) way. So, if in Hosea 4:6, God says "My people are destroyed from a lack of knowledge... ," and in John 10:10 Jesus tells us that the enemy, the antichrist's, the entity in direct opposition of what God stands for, mission is to steal, and to kill, and to destroy, is it safe to say that we, God's people (if you consider yourself as such), are easy pickings for the devil, because of ignorance?

"BOTH BLACK AND WHITE"

Tupac Shakur, one of the most outspoken and influential rappers ever, says in his song "Changes," "Cause both black and white are smoking crack tonight." He raises awareness that this is a problem we're all affected by. My question is: once you finish uplifting your race, what are you going to do about the others? What makes one race better than the others; what makes one racist better than the others? Nothing, there's no difference. There's no difference between a black racist and a white racist. Whether from the past or today. I walk this earth just like everybody else, and I haven't made myself blind to anything. I still see and receive every part of racism that the next man sees and receives. The difference is the way we see and receive it, and I don't act blind to how we give it out. I see it as a demonic stronghold of ignorance, FOR WHOEVER ALLOWS IT TO BE A CRUTCH FOR THEM. Yeah, I was just as affected by all of the recent police actions that have happened that have made the news, and so many other instances that haven't made the news. I don't mean I have just been affected lightly. I mean in my bathroom crying, not wanting people to see my tears of anger and sadness. Even debating with some of my Christian brothers and sisters because I was mad and caught up in my feelings. Thinking they weren't getting it, because they hadn't taken them walks home and been bothered by the police from just being who we were, young black teens in a bad neighborhood. All the while they were just as directly affected, even though they hadn't taken those walks, but they were clearly seeing it for what it was spiritually. They could tell it was the enemy trying to stir up something bigger like a race war or something that would set us back a hundred years.

I already know that some people are sitting there like "let's go to war," but you can get totally annihilated in a war that you're not supposed to be in. 1 Kings 22 tells the story of a king that was determined to go to war, and having an ally, was prepared for war. The ally, being a believer, wanted to know from God whether they should be going to war or not. So, the one king called on his prophets, a bunch of false prophets (around 400) that would prophesy to him what he wanted to hear, and of course that's what they did. They even did so in God's name. 1 Kings 22:6 (KJV), "Go up; for the Lord shall deliver it into the hand of the king." The other king, evidently seeing the bogusness in what was going on, asked for a different prophet of the Lord, and that prophet prophesied differently. He prophesied destruction of the kingdom and death to the king. He prophesied straight from God, whether it was going to be liked by the king or not, and it landed that prophet in prison. Not only did they not listen, but one of the prophets that the king had around him smacked the true prophet (1 Kings 22:24 MSG) saying "Since when did the Spirit of GOD leave me and take up with you?" Of course, they didn't listen, went to war, and sure enough everything happened just like he prophesied it would happen. You know what's crazy about that story, it was a deceiving spirit that convinced them to go to war. It's bigger than guns and things, but I understand.

See, the funny thing is that the king who wanted to go to war knew who this prophet was and that he was a true prophet of God, but because he never prophesied anything that he wanted to hear, he didn't want to call on him. The ally, who was also a king, wanted to hear a word from God. Here now, we hear a lot of people who will feed us what we want to hear based on our feelings, and it's happening when a lot of people's feelings are running high. A lot of false prophets that will play on our race and the things that's going on, and lead us down the wrong path. I'm like the ally, though. I want to hear a true word. I don't want it to be based on my feelings or theirs. I want it to be direction that's based off of God and not man.

I don't see God telling the African American race to go to war, anyway. He's trying to teach us something much bigger. He's trying to teach us something greater: forgiveness and love. If we learn forgiveness and love, we learn to allow God to work. Mathew 6:14 (KJV), "For if ye forgive men their trespasses, your heavenly Father will also forgive you."

The war we fight is spiritual, and it starts with ourselves. Until we can forgive, we will forever be corrupted to the core with bitterness. Hebrews 12:14-15 (NIV) , "Make every effort to live in peace with everyone and to be holy; without holiness no one will see the Lord. [15] See to it that no one falls short of the grace of God and that no bitter root grows up to cause trouble and defile many." Ephesians 4:31-32 (KJV), "Let all bitterness, and wrath, and anger, and clamour, and evil speaking, be put away from you, with all malice: ³² And be ye kind one to another, tenderhearted, forgiving one another, even as God for Christ's sake hath forgiven you." Bitterness will eat us from the inside. It will cause us to make unwise decisions. It will cause us to be UNFORGIVEN! It will turn us away from God. Not only turn us away from God, but provoke God to anger, through jealousy, by choosing other gods. Look closely, people are turning this way and that way all over the nation, and the stem of a lot of those decisions is a seed of hate that has been allowed to mature and take root in us. Who wants to give anyone or anything that type of control over them?

Ephesians 6:12 (KJV), "For we wrestle not against flesh and blood, but against principalities, against powers, against the rulers of the darkness of this world, against spiritual wickedness in high places." The white man is not the enemy, nor any other race for that matter, but more so anyone of any color, race, or origin who wants to keep racism abreast. Romans 12:21 (KJV) says, "Be not overcome with evil, but overcome evil with good." Having pride doesn't mean you have to hate another race. If that was the case then what makes us different from Hitler, or any other oppressor? Sports teams have pride in their team, but it doesn't have to cause them to have hate for any other team. Though, it can, and sometimes does for different reasons. If (and when) it does, that's when it has gone overboard.

How long will we allow hatred to control us? I'll let you in on a little secret: whenever a person can control when and where you get mad, they can control you. That's a tough lesson I had to learn for myself, and it has helped me a lot. Not that I don't still get angry, but I try not to let it control me. How long will you allow others to control you? Control your moves; control when you move and how you move? Then these false leaders, whether entertainers, religious or non-religious, play on those feelings that are bubbling at the surface or already spilling over. They play on the fact that the people already feel some kind of way. People are following because when we're in our feelings, it's easier for us to do exactly what 2 Timothy 4:3 said about following our own desires and finding teachers who give us what our itching ears want to hear. You will be just like me as that young 19-year-old boy being led astray because I was in my feelings. How are these leaders (if that's what you see them as) not being used by the enemy? I don't need you to tell me "we haven't made any progress." That's not a Godly word to me, and it's bogus. We can make all the comparisons and whatever else, I haven't been whipped as a slave, and I've never endured what they went through back then, not even what they went through in the early-to-mid 1900s. I don't need you to tell me "we need our own" or "we need to separate." No, we need to all be able to come together and make this thing work. That's not a Godly word to me. "We need to spend money with our own," that's not a Godly word to me. If a person is African American and a crook and only out to line his pockets, then what difference would it make if I spend money with him just because we are of the same race? On the other hand, if a person is ANY race, and his heart is in the right place, then we can work together to make anything better. That's one of the reason's we have to be in touch spiritually. Whether it is communities, schools, businesses, people, etc. With that said, that's where I want to spend my money! Proverbs 29:2 (NLV), "When those who are right with God rule, the people are glad, but when a sinful man rules, the people have sorrow."

When I speak on forgiveness, I speak from first hand experiences that many of the people that are pushing hate have never had to endure. I've had a police officer sit on my back with a gun to the back of my head, and while I was totally still, tell me if I moved again he was going to shoot me in the head, among the numerous other times I've had guns drawn on me. I somehow always fit the description of the so-called call they just received or the report they just got of a break in or someone selling drugs or whatever story they wanted to make up at the time. I've had my hands on the front of hot police cars, and sat on the side of the curb like a spectacle. I've been wrestled to the ground, slammed on the ground, tackled to the ground, and whatever else. I've had handcuffs put on so tight they felt like razor blades, only to be released and told to have a good night.

I was also on a panel, when the Mike Brown incident happened, telling the police about it when he tried to act totally oblivious to what's taking place in our neighborhoods between the people and the police. The last time I was arrested, when the police pulled me over, the first thing he told me was get out of the car, even while I was trying to hand him my valid driver's license.

With all of the things I've been through, place that on top of all the things I've witnessed, heard, and seen since a kid, I could take the hate that it had caused for most of my life, let it become a cancerous type of bitterness that I take to the grave, and who could blame me? Or I can practice Godly principles and forgive. Not just because someone told me to, but because truth be told, forgiving agrees with who I am. It agrees with who we are. I can be the bigger person. On top of that, we get the win. Nobody has control over us. Nobody pushes buttons and decides when, where, and how we react. Also, my forgiveness is locked in my ability to forgive. That's how we receive forgiveness!

JOHN 10:10 PT 2

"I am come that they might have life, and that they might have it more abundantly." The life we seek is not out there! When I say out there, I mean in the streets. While I was running the streets, I kicked, scratched, and scraped for every nickel. Now, some have it better, and truth be told I have had some good times. The good times don't outweigh the bad times in that field, though, and even the good times are infused with the stress that come with the lifestyle. An example of that is the fact that even if I buy something nice, there's the possibility that it could be taken because I didn't obtain it legally. The constant looking over your shoulder for the cops. The constant "over the shoulder" for enemies, or robbers, or "homeboys" who are right beside you, but mean you no good, or who's going to tell on you.

So many of us find the lives of gangsters that have misled us and continue to mislead us down a road that's trying to kill us, more fascinating than the life of the one that wants us to have life. YouTube is full of documentaries of old gangsters, new gangsters, any variety of gangster that we want to see. Every day they get more and more views; we're fascinated by the lives of gangsters. The stories of those that made it, even if for a brief moment, because the enemy has tricked us into believing that we don't deserve those things, we can't get those things because of our circumstances, or the only way to get it is by going the street route. So, if that is the only way then we celebrate those who made it.

Let's be honest and look at it from a different angle: Not all of "White America" has what they have because of "white privilege." Getting caught up on whether or not it exists is not my aim. Ask any of those hardworking white men and women how much they had to put in to make it. How many losses they had to take? How much sleep they had to miss out on, or time they had to sacrifice away from their families to make what they have a reality. Ask some of those who didn't have any of what they have handed down to them, who had to come up with the money all by themselves. Ask some of them who had to work to keep it. They had to put work in, just like anyone else. If you really want to be real, ask a white man or woman who hasn't been privy to white privilege at all.

Why did I say all of that? Well, one reason is because I want to move away from the excuses we use regarding white America as it relates to why we don't make it, even if the excuse is valid. Those excuses, valid or not, hasn't gotten anyone anywhere. If that's the case, why would I keep presenting them as if the excuses are something to stand on, and why in the world would I want to keep handing them down to the next generations? Another reason is because the difference is those that did make it believed they deserved it. No matter what anybody said! That's where people have to be spiritually, and mentally, and physically (and whatever else) in order to achieve the goals they are trying to reach. We have to believe that we deserve it. God has promised it to us! And we don't have to break the rules to get it, that's a dummy we're accepting.

How do I know we deserve it? Well, God promised it to us. How I do know that God promised it to us? Look at this: The Lord shall increase you more and more, you and your children. Psalm 115:14 KJV

The lions may grow weak and hungry but those who seek the Lord lack no good thing. Psalm 34:10 NIV

The blessing of the Lord brings wealth, without painful toil for it. Proverbs 10:22 NIV

The Lord will open the heavens, the storehouse of his bounty, to send rain on your land in season and to bless all the work of your hands. You will lend to many nations but will borrow from none. 13 The Lord will make you the head, not the tail. If you pay attention to the commands of the Lord your God I give you this day and carefully follow them, you will always be at the top, never at the bottom. Deuteronomy 28:12-13 NIV

I can give you a bunch of scriptures that tell you how good God is, or all about the promises of the Lord.. I'd rather stay with the one we were talking about from the jump, John 10:10. I'd rather concentrate on the fact that Jesus himself says he came that we may have life and that more abundantly. I'd rather magnify the word abundantly. Let's look at it together.

Abundance

Abundance means a large amount of something: abundant amount of something. Abundance means an ample quantity: profusion (great quantity; lavish display or supply). Abundance means affluence, wealth. Abundance means a relative degree of plentifulness.

Jesus came so that we can have life in that matter. In

fact, he made sure it was pointed out, "I am come that they might have life, and that they might have it more abundantly." He had already mentioned life, and he doubled back so that he could point out how he meant for that life to be. Have a life that's plentiful. Have a life that's affluent and wealthy. Have ample quantities. So, in actuality, Jesus came so that we might have everything that the enemy tricked us into thinking we could get from him. So, the enemy is selling us [a] false reality. The enemy is selling us a false substance. Now you tell me, is that not a dummy?

The greatest dummy ever sold was to Eve (and Adam). Even though they were in Eden and had a firsthand relationship, the devil convinced them there was something better, and was able to make them buy into the trick. God said "If you eat from the tree you will surely die." The devil disguised as a serpent said, "You won't surely die." Like I touched on, he was able to convince them that if they did it another way (any way other than God's way is the wrong way!!!) that they would somehow get more out of it than what they were getting through God while doing it the right way. Immediately, things switched for them, and not only for them, for us now. They experienced some things they never would've had to experience, had they not done wrong. Modern day terminology: "If you do this you'll die and go to hell."

Then the devil disguised as your brother, says "If you do this, bruh, you'll live. They just tell you that because they don't want you to live like them. I'm trying to eat." Don't get lost because I say your brother, but don't get fooled thinking it can't be your brother, sister, homie, friend, boyfriend, girlfriend, whatever. The enemy tried to use Jesus' disciple Peter against Jesus, and it was out of care. It was out of an honest place that Peter spoke, a passionate place, but anything that will make you deviate from the path that God has for you is not of God. So, Jesus had to rebuke Peter. In Matthew 16:23, Jesus turned and said to Peter, "Get behind me, Satan! You are a stumbling block to me; you do not have in mind the concerns of God, but merely human concerns." Nothing could be truer when someone is trying to get you to do something outside of what God wants you to do.

Could it be that we are experiencing some things that we never would've had to, had we stuck to doing things God's way? Just like the wrongs of Adam and Eve had future implications, what about ours? Will our kids' lives be impacted by the right or wrong we did yesterday, or those we do today or tomorrow? We've fallen for the same trick or bought the same dummy they bought in the garden thinking we would get something better by doing it outside of God; God's way; the righteous way; the right way!

THE DEVIL SOLD US A DUMMY

"Let the wicked forsake his way and the unrighteous man his thoughts; and let him return to the Lord, and He will have love, pity, and mercy for him, and to our God, for He will multiply to him His abundant pardon."

Isaiah 55:7

OMEGA

To All Who Know Me,

I'm talking about those who really know me....who have been around me out there. Not just been in my presence, but really been around me, young or old. I don't want you to forget who and how I was. I don't say this for street fame or glory, I say this so you can understand my total faith in The Lord. So you can understand my total trust in what He can do. Please remember it all, so that this can be real to you.

I say this because I recognize that when I tell my

testimony at times, all people see is the changed person, and they overlook the power of what has happened. Though that may be the case, I believe in scripture. So, I believe that my testimony shall help people overcome as I have overcame.

You guys witnessed my testimony, you are a part of it. Remember the good, remember the bad, remember the ugly. Know that this wasn't just a decision that I made that changed my life, because truth is, my decision was to run the streets, and deal with whatever the outcome was to be. Whether it was death or jail, which is usually the outcome for everyone we know.

You all hold a special place in my heart! You're the reason the book ever came about. As it formed in my mind, I realized that it may be beneficial for more than just the people from my neighborhood, but to people everywhere that would be able to relate.

My prayer is to see my whole neighborhood living under the sound counsel of God. My prayer is that we are the example for the city, that our city is an example for the state, and that our state is the prototype for the country. That we policed ourselves.

My prayer is that years from now, we're showing up at our children's graduations as accomplished men and women. In that we will know that we have defied the odds! In that we will be able to tell the next person that

God is real, and be able to tell them how real He is. It will have substance because we will know that we were too crazy to come out of all that alone.

If you're not getting what I'm saying, I'm still you! When I say I'm still you, I mean that if you haven't up and got your life together, then why would you think that I could, on my own? You saw how I was, how messed up I was, how possessed by what was going on I was. I didn't change on my own, I pulled on God! I'm only where I am now because of God! He chose me! He chose me for a reason. I went through everything I went through for a reason. I went through for you. I went through it so that y'all could see someone that far in. Someone that messed up in the head. Someone that controlled be the theatrics of the street. Someone that almost everybody had counted out, because all the odds were stacked against me. Someone that, at one time, if you hung around me no one could understand why, you probably didn't at some time or another.

Even in the mist of all that I feel/felt like I stood for principle, but even most of that was twisted street principle. You had to see someone that was so far in that there was no way out. So, He could pull me out, and you could see it. So, He gets all the glory! So you will know who to pull on! Just like He chose me, He chose you too. So that we can be an example for someone else. 1

Timothy 1:15-17 (NIV), "Here is a trustworthy saying that deserves full acceptance: Christ Jesus came into the world to save sinners—of whom I am the worst. [16] But for that very reason I was shown mercy so that in me, the worst of sinners, Christ Jesus might display his immense patience as an example for those who would believe in him and receive eternal life. [17] Now to the King eternal, immortal, invisible, the only God, be honor and glory for ever and ever. Amen." Let this be the platform you need to help someone else. Let this be the platform you need so that our kids get to see a different lifestyle. So that we are not the ones leading them to destruction. So we're not the ones selling them a dummy.

P.S. I unapologetically used Scripture throughout this book to back what I have written.

"I consider that our present sufferings are not worth comparing with the glory that will be revealed in us. For the creation waits in eager expectation for the children of God to be revealed. For the creation was subjected to frustration, not by its own choice, but by the will of the one who subjected it, in hope that[h] the creation itself will be liberated from its bondage to decay and brought into the freedom and glory of the children of God.

We know that the whole creation has been groaning as in the pains of childbirth right up to the present time. Not only so, but we ourselves, who have the firstfruits of the Spirit, groan inwardly as we wait eagerly for our adoption to sonship, the redemption of our bodies. For in this hope we were saved. But hope that is seen is no hope at all. Who hopes for what they already have? But if we hope for what we do not yet have, we wait for it patiently."

Romans 8:18-25

ABOUT THE AUTHOR

Stewart Brockenbrough grew up in Richmond, Virginia. He now lives in Baltimore, Maryland, where he works as a Treatment Coordinator at Helping Up Mission. You can connect with Stu via his website:

www.thegoodstewart.com

Made in the USA
Lexington, KY
14 March 2017